101 THINGS® TO DO WITH

RAMEN
NOODLES

101 THINGS® TO DO WITH
RAMEN
NOODLES

TONI PATRICK

Gibbs Smith

Second Edition
27 26 25 24 23   6 5 4 3 2

First Gibbs Smith edition published in 2005
Second Gibbs Smith edition published May 2023

Published by
Gibbs Smith, Publisher
P.O. Box 667
Layton, Utah 84041

1.800.835.4993 orders
www.gibbs-smith.com

Designed by Ryan Thomann and Renee Bond
Printed and bound in China
Gibbs Smith books are printed on either recycled, 100% post-consumer
waste, FSC-certified papers or on paper produced from sustainable PEFC-
certified forest/controlled wood source. Learn more at www.pefc.org.

Library of Congress has cataloged the first edition as follows:
Patrick, Toni.
101 things to do with ramen noodles / Toni Patrick.—1st ed.
p. cm.
ISBN : 978-1-58685-735-6 (first edition)
1. Cookery (Pasta) 2. Noodles. I. Title: One hundred one things to do with ramen
noodles. II. Title: One hundred and one things to do with ramen noodles. III. Title.
TX809.M17P376 2005
641.8'22—dc22
2005002259

ISBN 978-1-4236-6374-4

This book is dedicated to my mother. If it weren't
for her threatening to steal my idea and do
the book herself, I wouldn't have done it.
I love you, Mom,

CONTENTS

Helpful Hints

- Your freezer is your friend. When buying meat, divide into individual portions and freeze in zipper-lock plastic bags. Buy large bags of frozen vegetables and use portions as needed. Freeze all leftovers; days will come when your pocket is empty or restaurants are closed.

- When using vegetables, canned, fresh, and frozen are interchangeable, unless specified. And remember, canned food doesn't spoil until after it has been opened.

- Macaroni can be used in place of ramen noodles.

- Save all extra seasoning packets for future use. Sprinkle a seasoning packet over hamburger or chicken and brown together for a great flavor.

- Macaroni cheese packets can be used in place of real cheese.

- Two tablespoons dehydrated minced or chopped onion is equal to $\frac{1}{4}$ cup fresh minced onion.

- Salt lovers beware. Before adding extra salt, taste your food. Seasoning packets are always salty.

- To cook noodles, follow the directions on the package unless recipe says otherwise.

- Add more or less of any ingredient to your own liking. Be creative and enjoy yourself.

- Low-fat or light soups, sour cream, and cream cheese can be substituted if you prefer.

SOUPS

Minestrone

MAKES 2 SERVINGS

1 package	ramen noodles, any flavor
1 can (10.75 ounces)	condensed tomato soup
8 ounces	cooked spicy smoked sausage, thinly sliced
¼ cup	cooked sliced celery
¼ cup	cooked sliced carrots
¼ cup	peas
½ cup	green beans
½ cup	canned kidney beans, drained and rinsed
	salt and pepper, to taste

Cook noodles in water according to package directions. Do not drain. Add soup, sausage, and vegetables. Simmer 5–10 minutes, or until vegetables are tender. Add more water by tablespoon if soup is too thick. Season with salt and pepper.

Egg Drop Soup

MAKES 2 SERVINGS

2 cups	**water**
1 package	**chicken ramen noodles, with seasoning packet**
2	**eggs, beaten**
¼ cup	**diced onion**
¼ cup	**diced celery**
¼ cup	**diced green bell pepper**

In a saucepan, bring water to boiling and add seasoning packet, eggs, and vegetables. Stir constantly until eggs look done. Simmer 5 minutes. Add noodles and cook 3–5 minutes more, or until noodles are tender.

Beefed-Up Noodles

MAKES 2 SERVINGS

2 cups	**water**
⅛ cup	**diced onion**
⅛ cup	**sliced carrots**
⅛ cup	**diced celery**
1 sprig	**parsley**
1 small	**bay leaf**
⅛ teaspoon	**thyme leaves**
1 package	**beef ramen noodles, with seasoning packet**

In a saucepan, heat all ingredients except noodles and seasoning packet to boiling. Add seasoning packet. Reduce heat and simmer 30 minutes. Strain liquid into a separate container. Add noodles to liquid and cook 3 minutes, or until noodles are done.

Chicken Consommé and Noodles

MAKES 2 SERVINGS

2 cups	water
⅛ cup	diced onion
⅛ cup	sliced carrots
⅛ cup	diced celery
1 sprig	parsley
1 small	bay leaf
⅛ teaspoon	thyme leaves
1 package	chicken ramen noodles, with seasoning packet

In a saucepan, heat all ingredients except noodles and seasoning packet to boiling. Add seasoning packet. Reduce heat and simmer 30 minutes. Strain liquid into a separate container. Add noodles to liquid and cook 3 minutes, or until noodles are done.

Creamy Chicken Noodle Soup

MAKES 2 SERVINGS

1 package	chicken ramen noodles, with seasoning packet
1 can (10.75 ounces)	condensed cream of chicken soup
½ cup	diced onion
½ cup	sliced carrots
½ cup	sliced celery

Cook noodles in water according to package directions and drain.

Prepare soup as directed on can. Add seasoning packet and vegetables to soup. Cook over medium heat 5–10 minutes, or until vegetables are tender. Add noodles and simmer 2–3 minutes more.

Creamy Mushroom Soup
MAKES 2 SERVINGS

1 package	**ramen noodles, any flavor**
1 can (10.75 ounces)	**condensed cream of mushroom soup**
1 cup	**sliced fresh mushrooms**
	salt and pepper, to taste

Cook noodles in water according to package directions and drain.

Prepare soup as directed on can. Mix noodles and soup together. Add mushrooms and simmer 5 minutes. Season with salt and pepper.

Tomato Noodle Soup

MAKES 2 SERVINGS

1 package	**ramen noodles, any flavor**
1 can (10.75 ounces)	**condensed tomato soup**

Cook noodles in water according to package directions. Do not drain. Add soup. Simmer 5 minutes, stirring occasionally.

Vegetable Beef Noodle Soup

MAKES 2–4 SERVINGS

¾ pound	ground beef
1 cup	chopped tomatoes
½ cup	chopped carrots
½ cup	chopped celery
4 cups	water
2 packages	beef ramen noodles, with seasoning packets

In a frying pan, brown and drain beef. Add vegetables, water, and seasoning packets. Bring to a boil and simmer 20 minutes. Add noodles and cook 3 minutes more, or until noodles are done.

Summer Garden Soup

MAKES 2–4 SERVINGS

½ cup	chopped onion
1 cup	julienned zucchini
½ cup	chopped carrots
¼ cup	butter or margarine
1 teaspoon	basil
2 packages	beef ramen noodles, with seasoning packets
4 cups	water
1 cup	green beans
1 cup	chopped tomatoes

In a frying pan, cook onion, zucchini, and carrots in butter and basil over medium heat until vegetables are tender.

In a saucepan, combine cooked vegetables, noodles, water, green beans, tomatoes, and seasoning packets. Heat to boiling and simmer 5 minutes.

Southwest Vegetable Soup

MAKES 2 SERVINGS

1 can (10.75 ounces)	**condensed tomato soup**
1 cup	**water**
1 can (10.75 ounces)	**enchilada sauce**
½ cup	**corn**
½ cup	**green beans**
½ cup	**canned kidney beans, drained and rinsed**
½ cup	**salsa**
½ cup	**chopped cooked chicken**
1 package	**ramen noodles, any flavor, crumbled**
	tortilla chips
	Monterey Jack cheese, grated

In a soup pot, combine tomato soup, water, and enchilada sauce. Cook over medium heat until hot. Add vegetables, salsa, and chicken. Simmer 15 minutes. Add crumbled noodles and simmer 3–5 minutes more. Serve topped with chips and cheese.

Asian-Inspired Beef Noodle Soup

MAKES 4–6 SERVINGS

1 pound	ground beef, browned and drained
1	medium onion, chopped
1 tablespoon	minced garlic
1 teaspoon	ground ginger
5 cups	water
1	medium head bok choy
2 packages	beef ramen noodles, with seasoning packets
1½ teaspoons	canola oil
2 tablespoons	soy sauce

In a 4-quart soup pot, combine cooked beef, onion, garlic, ginger, and water, and bring to a boil. Stir in bok choy. Simmer over medium heat 3 minutes. Break noodles in half and stir into soup. Simmer 3–5 minutes more, or until noodles are done. Stir in seasoning packets, oil, and soy sauce.

To prepare bok choy for use, rinse with cold water, cut off the very bottom of the stems and discard. Cut remaining bok choy into bite-size pieces.

SALADS

Spring Salad

MAKES 2–4 SERVINGS

2 packages	**chicken ramen noodles, with seasoning packets**
2 teaspoons	**sesame oil**
3 tablespoons	**lemon juice**
⅓ cup	**vegetable oil**
2 teaspoons	**sugar**
1 cup	**halved red and/or green seedless grapes**
½ cup	**diced red and/or green apple**
½ cup	**diced pineapple chunks**
3 tablespoons	**chopped green onion**
8 ounces	**smoked turkey breast, cut into strips**
¼ cup	**walnut pieces**

Cook noodles in water according to package directions and drain. Rinse with cold water. Add sesame oil and refrigerate.

For dressing, combine lemon juice, vegetable oil, seasoning packets, and sugar. Pour over noodles. Then add grapes, apple, pineapple, onion, turkey, and walnut pieces. Toss to coat.

Summer Picnic Salad

MAKES 2 SERVINGS

1 package	**ramen noodles, any flavor, broken up**
¼ cup	**alfalfa sprouts**
½ cup	**peas**
	French dressing

Cook noodles in water according to package directions and drain. Top with alfalfa sprouts and peas. Mix with desired amount of dressing.

Antipasto Salad

MAKES 2–4 SERVINGS

2 packages	**ramen noodles, any flavor**
¾ cup	**cubed pepperoni**
½ cup	**sliced black olives**
¼ cup	**sliced onion**
	Italian dressing

Cook noodles in water according to package directions and drain. Add pepperoni, olives, and onion. Drizzle desired amount of dressing over top and toss to coat.

Zucchini Salad

MAKES 2 SERVINGS

1 package	ramen noodles, any flavor
½ cup	chopped zucchini
½ cup	chopped carrots
⅛ cup	sliced olives
1 teaspoon	Dijon mustard
½ teaspoon	basil
¼ teaspoon	oregano
¼ teaspoon	garlic powder
2 tablespoons	vinegar

Cook noodles in water according to package directions and drain. Add vegetables to noodles. In a small bowl, mix together mustard, spices, and vinegar. Add to noodle mixture and toss to coat.

Taco Salad

MAKES 2–4 SERVINGS

2 packages	**beef ramen noodles, with seasoning packets**
1 pound	**ground beef, browned and drained**
1 large	**tomato, chopped**
¾ cup	**chopped onion**
2 cups	**grated cheddar cheese**
	Thousand Island dressing or salsa

Cook noodles in water according to package directions and drain.

In a large bowl, stir 1 seasoning packet into cooked beef. Add tomato, onion, and cheese. Spoon mixture over warm noodles and drizzle with dressing or salsa.

Three-Bean Salad

MAKES 2 SERVINGS

1 package	ramen noodles, any flavor
½ cup	green beans
½ cup	canned kidney beans, drained and rinsed
½ cup	canned lima beans, drained and rinsed
¼ cup	Italian dressing
	salt and pepper, to taste

Cook noodles in water according to package directions and drain. Add beans and stir in dressing. Season with salt and pepper.

Pasta Salad

MAKES 2 SERVINGS

1 package	ramen noodles, any flavor, with seasoning packet
$\frac{1}{2}$ cup	mayonnaise
1 tablespoon	mustard
$1\frac{1}{2}$ teaspoons	honey
1	celery stalk, chopped
$\frac{1}{4}$ cup	cubed cheddar cheese
2	hard-boiled eggs, chopped

Cook noodles in water according to package directions and drain. In a large bowl, mix mayonnaise, mustard, and honey with $\frac{1}{2}$ of the seasoning packet. Add noodles, celery, cheese, and eggs. Toss gently to coat.

Water Chestnut Ramen Salad

MAKES 4–6 SERVINGS

4 packages	**chicken ramen noodles, with seasoning packets**
1 cup	**diced celery**
1 can (8 ounces)	**sliced water chestnuts, drained**
1 cup	**chopped red onion**
1 cup	**diced green bell pepper**
1 cup	**peas**
1 cup	**mayonnaise**

Break each package of noodles into 4 pieces. Cook noodles in water according to package directions, then drain and rinse with cold water.

In a large bowl, stir noodles, celery, water chestnuts, onion, pepper, and peas together. In a medium bowl, combine mayonnaise and 3 seasoning packets. Fold mayonnaise mixture into salad. Cover and refrigerate at least 1 hour before serving.

Chicken Salad with Almonds and Sesame Seeds

MAKES 2–4 SERVINGS

1 package	ramen noodles, any flavor
1 teaspoon	vinegar
½ cup	oil
3 teaspoons	seasoned salt
½ teaspoon	pepper
3 tablespoons	sugar
4 cups	shredded cooked chicken breast
3 to 6	green onions, sliced
¾ cup	sliced celery
¼ cup	sesame seeds
1 cup	slivered almonds
½	head lettuce, torn or shredded

Cook noodles in water for 1 minute and drain.

In a large bowl, mix vinegar, oil, salt, pepper, and sugar. Add chicken, onions, celery, and sesame seeds. Add prepared noodles and roasted almonds. Add lettuce just before serving and toss.

For more flavor, roast the almonds in a 350 degree oven for about 10 minutes until lightly browned, stirring every couple of minutes to avoid burning.

Fruity Ramen Salad

MAKES 2 SERVINGS

Dressing:

½ teaspoon	salt
dash	pepper
1 teaspoon	vegetable oil
1 tablespoon	chopped parsley
2 tablespoons	sugar
2 tablespoons	vinegar
dash	vinegar hot sauce, such as Tabasco

Salad:

1 package	ramen noodles, any flavor
½ cup	slivered almonds
2 tablespoons	sugar
1 cup	diced cooked ham
1 can (10 ounces)	mandarin oranges, drained

In a small bowl, combine dressing ingredients and set aside.

Cook noodles in water according to package directions, then drain and rinse with cold water.

In a frying pan, lightly brown almonds and sugar over medium heat, stirring constantly so almonds are coated in sugar.

In a large bowl, mix ham, oranges, and noodles. Add dressing and toss to coat. Just before serving, add almonds and toss again.

Sweet-and-Sour Salad
MAKES 6–8 SERVINGS

1 cup	canola or olive oil
½ cup	sugar
½ cup	apple cider vinegar
1 tablespoon	soy sauce
½ cup	butter
1 cup	chopped walnuts
1 package	ramen noodles, any flavor, crushed
1 head	romaine lettuce
4 cups	chopped fresh broccoli
½ cup	chopped green onions

In a medium bowl, combine oil, sugar, vinegar, and soy sauce together. Cover and refrigerate overnight.

In a saucepan, melt butter over medium heat. Stir walnuts and noodles into butter. Stir until heated.

Tear lettuce into bite-size pieces and place in a large bowl. Add broccoli and onions. Pour dressing over top and toss to coat. Sprinkle walnut-ramen mixture over salad.

BEEF

Beef Ramenoff

MAKES 2 SERVINGS

½ pound	beef strips
2 cups	sour cream
1 tablespoon	chopped chives
1 teaspoon	salt
⅛ teaspoon	pepper
1	garlic clove, crushed
½ cup	grated Parmesan cheese, divided
1 packages	ramen noodles, any flavor
2 tablespoons	butter or margarine

In a frying pan, brown beef until done. Add sour cream, spices, and ¼ cup Parmesan, and simmer over low heat.

Cook noodles in water according to package directions and drain. Stir butter into warm noodles until melted. Fold in beef mixture. Sprinkle with remaining ¼ cup cheese.

Creamy Beef and Broccoli Noodles

MAKES 2 SERVINGS

³⁄₄ **pound**	**beef sirloin, cubed**
¹⁄₂ **teaspoon**	**garlic powder**
1	**onion, cut into wedges**
2 cups	**broccoli pieces**
1 can (10.75 ounces)	**condensed cream of broccoli soup**
¹⁄₄ **cup**	**water**
1 tablespoon	**soy sauce**
2 packages	**beef ramen noodles, with seasoning packets**

In a frying pan, brown beef with garlic powder until done. Stir in onion and broccoli. Cook over medium heat until vegetables are tender. Add soup, water, and soy sauce. Simmer 10 minutes.

Cook noodles in water according to package directions and drain. Add seasoning packets. Serve beef mixture over warm noodles.

Beef Provençal

MAKES 2 SERVINGS

1 pound	beef strips
1 package	beef ramen noodles, with seasoning packet
1 cup	water
2 tablespoons	butter or margarine
1	onion, sliced
2 tablespoons	flour
1	tomato, chopped
1 can (4 ounces)	sliced mushrooms, drained
1 teaspoon	garlic powder

In a frying pan, brown beef until done.

In a small bowl, mix together seasoning packet and water.

In a saucepan, heat butter until golden brown. Add onion and cook until tender, then discard onion. Stir in flour, over low heat, until brown. Remove from heat. Add water mixture and heat to boiling, stirring constantly for 1 minute. Gently stir in tomato, mushrooms, and garlic powder.

Cook noodles in water according to package directions and drain.

Top warm noodles with beef and sauce.

Marinated Beef

MAKES 2 SERVINGS

¾ pound	beef strips
1 package	beef ramen noodles, with seasoning packet
½ cup	water
2 tablespoons	oil
¼ cup	sliced green onion
1 tablespoon	butter or margarine
1 can (14.5 ounces)	diced tomatoes, drained

In a large bowl, marinate beef in seasoning packet, water, and oil for 30 minutes. In a frying pan, cook beef in marinade until done. Add onion and butter, and sauté 5 minutes.

Cook noodles in water according to package directions and drain. Add tomatoes and cooked noodles to beef mixture. Simmer 5–10 minutes, or until heated through.

Cheddar and Beef Casserole

MAKES 2–4 SERVINGS

2 packages	beef ramen noodles, with seasoning packets
1 pound	ground beef
½ cup	sliced celery
¼ cup	chopped green bell pepper
½ cup	chopped onion
3 cups	grated cheddar cheese
2 cups	corn
1 can (6 ounces)	tomato paste
½ cup	water

Preheat oven to 350 degrees.

Cook noodles in water according to package directions; drain and set aside.

In a frying pan, brown beef with celery, pepper, and onion. Set aside.

In a 2-quart casserole dish, mix remaining ingredients with 1 seasoning packet. Add beef mixture and noodles and toss to coat. Bake 15–20 minutes.

#28
Beef and Broccoli Stir-Fry
MAKES 2–4 SERVINGS

1 pound	beef strips
1 tablespoon	oil
2 packages	beef ramen noodles, with seasoning packets
2 cups	broccoli pieces
1 cup	green onions, cut into strips
2 tablespoons	soy sauce
$\frac{1}{4}$ teaspoon	crushed red pepper

In a frying pan, brown and drain beef. Add oil, 1 seasoning packet, broccoli, and onions. Stir-fry 5 minutes. Add soy sauce and red pepper. Simmer 5 minutes more.

Cook noodles in water according to package directions and drain. Serve beef mixture over warm noodles.

Ramen Burgers

MAKES 4 HAMBURGERS

1 package	**beef ramen noodles, with seasoning packet**
1 pound	**ground beef**
1	**egg**
4	**hamburger buns**

Cook noodles in water 1½ minutes and drain. Add beef, egg, and ½ of the seasoning packet. Mix well and form into four patties. Grill or cook 5 minutes per side, or until desired doneness.

Serve these with your favorite hamburger fixings, including lettuce, tomato, ketchup, and mustard.

#30

Cheeseburger Ramen

MAKES 2 SERVINGS

½ pound	**ground beef**
1 package	**beef ramen noodles, with seasoning packet**
1 cup	**grated cheddar cheese**
1	**tomato, diced, optional**

In a frying pan, brown and drain beef. Season to taste with ½ of the seasoning packet.

Cook noodles in water according to package directions and drain. Add beef and cheese to noodles and stir until cheese is melted. Add tomatoes, if desired.

Japanese-Style Beef and Noodles

MAKES 2–4 SERVINGS

2 packages	beef ramen noodles, with seasoning packets
1/2 cup	water
1 pound	beef strips
2 tablespoons	oil
2 tablespoons	sugar
1/2 cup	soy sauce
1 can (4 ounces)	sliced mushrooms, drained
1/2 cup	sliced green onions
1 cup	sliced onion
1	celery stalk, sliced
1 can (8 ounces)	bamboo shoots
3 cups	fresh spinach

In a small bowl, mix together 1/2 of 1 seasoning packet and water.

In a frying pan, brown beef in oil until done, then push to one side of the pan. Stir in water mixture, sugar, and soy sauce. Add mushrooms, green onion, onion, celery, bamboo shoots, and spinach and cook until tender. Cover and simmer 5 minutes. Stir together.

Cook noodles in water according to package directions and drain. Add remaining 1 1/2 seasoning packets. Serve beef mixture over warm noodles.

Beefy Mushroom Noodles
MAKES 2–4 SERVINGS

2 packages	**beef ramen noodles, with seasoning packets**
2 cups	**water**
1½ pounds	**beef strips**
¼ cup	**butter or margarine**
2 cans (4 ounces each)	**sliced mushrooms, drained**
¼ cup	**flour**
	Worcestershire sauce, to taste

Cook noodles in water according to package directions and drain.

In a medium bowl, mix together seasoning packets and water.

In a frying pan, brown and drain beef.

In a small saucepan, melt butter over low heat. Stir in mushrooms and brown slowly. Add flour and cook, stirring, until deep brown. Add water mixture. Heat to boiling and stir 1 minute. Add Worcestershire sauce. Top warm noodles with beef and sauce.

Vegetable Beef Noodles

MAKES 2 SERVINGS

½ pound	ground beef
1 can (8 ounces)	tomato sauce
2 cups	frozen mixed vegetables
1 package	beef ramen noodles, with seasoning packet

In a frying pan, brown and drain beef. Add tomato sauce, vegetables, and seasoning packet to cooked beef. Simmer 10 minutes, or until vegetables are tender.

Cook noodles in water according to package directions and drain. Add noodles to beef mixture and simmer 2–3 minutes.

Beef 'n' Potato Noodles

MAKES 2–4 SERVINGS

1 pound	ground beef
2 packages	beef ramen noodles, with seasoning packets
2 cups	cubed potatoes
2 cups	diced tomatoes

In a frying pan, brown beef with seasoning packets until done. Add potatoes and cook until tender.

Cook noodles in water according to package directions and drain. Stir in tomatoes, then add noodles and tomatoes to beef mixture and simmer 5 minutes.

Beefy Chili Noodles

MAKES 2–4 SERVINGS

1 pound	ground beef
2 packages	beef ramen noodles, with seasoning packets
2 cans (4 ounces each)	sliced mushrooms, drained
½ cup	chopped onion
½ cup	chopped tomato
1 can (15 ounces)	kidney beans, drained and rinsed
¼ teaspoon	chili powder
1 cup	water

In a frying pan, brown and drain beef. Add noodles, mushrooms, onion, tomato, kidney beans, chili powder, water, and 1 seasoning packet. Simmer 10 minutes or until noodles are done.

Spicy Beef Noodles

MAKES 2–4 SERVINGS

2 packages	**ramen noodles, any flavor, with seasoning packets**
½ pound	**ground beef**
½ pound	**ground spicy sausage**
½ cup	**diced onion**
¾ cup	**diced green bell pepper**
¾ cup	**salsa**

Cook noodles in water according to package directions; drain and set aside.

In a frying pan, brown beef and sausage together then drain. Add onion, pepper, and salsa. Cook until vegetables are tender. Add noodles and simmer 2–3 minutes.

Spicy Meat-and-Cheese Roll

MAKES 2–4 SERVINGS

1 pound	**ground beef**
1 package	**beef ramen noodles, crushed**
1 cup	**grated cheddar cheese**
½ cup	**salsa**

Preheat oven to 350 degrees.

Flatten beef into a ½-inch-thick rectangle in a baking dish. Sprinkle uncooked noodles over beef. Top with a layer of cheese. Roll from one end to the other and pinch ends to prevent cheese from melting to the outside. Transfer to a loaf pan, then top with salsa.

Bake 30 minutes. Top with more salsa before serving, if desired.

Country Vegetable Beef

MAKES 2–4 SERVINGS

2 cups	**water**
2 tablespoons	**cornstarch**
2 packages	**beef ramen noodles, with seasoning packets**
1 pound	**ground beef**
4 cups	**frozen mixed vegetables**

In a small saucepan, mix water, cornstarch, and seasoning packets. Stir constantly over low heat until mixture thickens.

In a frying pan, brown and drain beef. Add vegetables and cook until tender. Add gravy and stir.

Cook noodles in water according to package directions and drain. Serve gravy over warm noodles.

Beefy Noodles with Gravy

MAKES 2 SERVINGS

1 pound	beef strips
1 package	beef ramen noodles, with seasoning packet
1 envelope	brown gravy mix

In a frying pan, brown beef until done.

Cook noodles in water according to package directions; drain and set aside.

In a saucepan, prepare gravy according to package directions. Top warm noodles with beef and gravy.

CHICKEN

Creamy Chicken and Broccoli

MAKES 2–4 SERVINGS

3	boneless, skinless chicken breasts, cut into strips
2 cups	chopped fresh or frozen broccoli
2 cans (10.75 ounces each)	condensed cream of mushroom soup
2 packages	chicken ramen noodles, with seasoning packets

In a frying pan, brown chicken until done. Add broccoli and soup to chicken. Cook over medium heat until broccoli is tender. Add $\frac{1}{2}$ of 1 seasoning packet, or to taste.

Cook noodles in water according to package directions and drain. Serve chicken and broccoli mixture over warm noodles.

#41

Spicy Chicken

MAKES 2–4 SERVINGS

3	boneless, skinless chicken breasts, cut into strips
3/4 teaspoon	garlic powder
1 can (14.5 ounces)	diced tomatoes with green chilies, drained
1 cup	chopped green bell peppers
2 cups	water
2 packages	chicken ramen noodles, with seasoning packets

In a frying pan, brown chicken until done. Add garlic powder, tomatoes and chilies, peppers, water, and seasoning packets. Simmer 10 minutes. Add noodles and cook 3–5 minutes more.

Cheesy Chicken Divan

MAKES 2–4 SERVINGS

2 cups	fresh broccoli pieces
2 to 4	boneless, skinless chicken breasts, cut into chunks
2 packages	chicken ramen noodles
1 can (10.75 ounces)	condensed cream of chicken soup
¾ cup	mayonnaise
1 teaspoon	mild curry powder
	salt and pepper, to taste
1 cup	grated cheddar cheese

Preheat oven to 350 degrees.

Place broccoli in a saucepan and cover with water. Cook over medium heat until broccoli is tender. Drain and spread in a lightly greased 9 x 9-inch casserole dish.

In a frying pan, brown chicken until done. Spread chicken over broccoli.

Cook noodles in water according to package directions and drain. Spread noodles over broccoli and chicken.

Mix together soup, mayonnaise, curry powder, salt, and pepper. Spoon mixture over broccoli, chicken, and noodles; sprinkle with cheese and bake 30 minutes.

Easy Chicken Allemande

MAKES 2 SERVINGS

2	boneless, skinless chicken breasts, cut into chunks
2 packages	chicken ramen noodles, with seasoning packets
1 cup	water
2 tablespoons	flour
	salt and pepper, to taste
1/8 teaspoon	nutmeg
1	egg yolk
2 tablespoons	butter or margarine, melted
2 tablespoons	heavy cream
1 teaspoon	lemon juice

In a frying pan, brown chicken until done.

Cook noodles in water according to package directions and drain.

In a small bowl, mix together water and 1 seasoning packet.

In a saucepan, mix flour, salt, pepper, and nutmeg together. Beat egg yolk into water mixture, and then stir into flour mixture. Heat to boiling and boil 1 minute, stirring constantly. Remove from heat. Stir in butter, cream, and lemon juice. Add chicken and simmer 2–3 minutes. Top warm noodles with chicken and sauce.

Chicken "Lo Mein"

MAKES 2 SERVINGS

1 tablespoon	oil
1 tablespoon	soy sauce
1 package	chicken ramen noodles, with seasoning packet
1 pound	boneless, skinless chicken breasts, cut into strips
½ cup	sliced onion
½ cup	chopped green bell pepper
¼ cup	chopped carrot

In a frying pan, mix oil, soy sauce, and ½ of the seasoning packet. Add chicken and brown until done. Add vegetables to chicken, and cook until tender.

Cook noodles in water according to package directions and drain. Add noodles to chicken and vegetables and cook over medium heat 3 minutes, stirring constantly.

Chicken Hollandaise

MAKES 2–4 SERVINGS

2 to 4	boneless, skinless chicken breasts, cut into chunks
2 packages	chicken ramen noodles, with seasoning packets
4	egg yolks
6 tablespoons	lemon juice
1 cup	butter or margarine

In a frying pan, brown chicken until done. Season with ½ of 1 seasoning packet, or to taste.

In a small saucepan, whisk egg yolks and lemon juice briskly with a fork. Add ½ cup butter and stir over low heat until melted. Add remaining butter, stirring briskly until butter melts and sauce thickens.

Cook noodles in water according to package directions and drain. Top warm noodles with chicken and sauce.

Chicken Ramen Velouté

MAKES 2 SERVINGS

1 pound	boneless, skinless chicken breasts, cut into chunks
1 cup	water
1 package	chicken ramen noodles, with seasoning packet
2 tablespoons	butter or margarine
2 tablespoons	flour
1/8 teaspoon	nutmeg

In a frying pan, brown chicken until done.

In a small bowl, mix together water and 1 seasoning packet.

In a saucepan, melt butter over low heat. Mix in flour, stirring until smooth and bubbly. Remove from heat. Stir in water mixture and nutmeg. Heat to boiling, stirring 1 minute. Add chicken and simmer over low heat until warmed through.

Cook noodles in water according to package directions and drain. Top warm noodles with chicken and sauce.

Chicken Curry

MAKES 2 SERVINGS

2	boneless, skinless chicken breasts
¼ cup	butter or margarine
¼ cup	flour
½ teaspoon	curry powder
2 packages	chicken ramen noodles, with seasoning packets
2 cups	milk

In a frying pan, brown chicken until done. Set aside.

In a small saucepan, melt butter. Stir in flour, curry powder, and 1 seasoning packet. Cook on low heat, stirring until smooth and bubbly. Add milk and heat to boiling, stirring 1 minute. Add chicken and simmer over low heat until warmed through.

Cook noodles in water according to package directions and drain. Top warm noodles with chicken and sauce.

Chicken with Creamy Herb Sauce

MAKES 2 SERVINGS

2	boneless, skinless chicken breasts, cut into chunks
1 package	chicken ramen noodles, with seasoning packet
1 cup	water
2 tablespoons	butter or margarine
2 tablespoons	flour
2 tablespoons	chopped onion
1 tablespoon	vinegar
1 tablespoon	chopped parsley
$\frac{1}{4}$ teaspoon	tarragon leaves
$\frac{1}{4}$ teaspoon	thyme leaves

In a frying pan, brown chicken until done. Cook noodles in water according to package directions; drain and set aside.

In a small bowl, mix together water and 1 seasoning packet.

In a small saucepan, heat butter over low heat until golden brown. Blend in flour, stirring until deep brown. Remove from heat. Add water mixture, onion, vinegar, and herbs, and heat to boiling, stirring 1 minute. Top warm noodles with chicken and sauce.

Creamy Chicken Noodles

MAKES 2 SERVINGS

1 package	**chicken ramen noodles, with seasoning packet**
1 can (10.75 ounces)	**condensed cream of chicken soup**
¼ cup	**diced onion**
1 can (5 ounces)	**chicken**

Cook noodles in water according to package directions and drain.

In a saucepan, heat soup, onion, chicken, and just under ½ of the seasoning packet over medium heat 5 minutes. Top warm noodles with soup mixture.

Chicken with Mushrooms

MAKES 2–4 SERVINGS

¹⁄₄ cup	butter or margarine
1 pound	boneless, skinless chicken tenders, cut into chunks
2 cups	sliced fresh mushrooms
2 packages	chicken ramen noodles, with seasoning packets

In a frying pan, melt butter and brown chicken until done. Add mushrooms and sauté 5 minutes, or until tender.

Cook noodles in water according to package directions and drain. Add 1 seasoning packet. Top warm noodles with chicken and mushrooms.

Chicken Alfredo

MAKES 2 SERVINGS

2	boneless, skinless chicken breasts, cut into strips
2 packages	ramen noodles, any flavor
1 cup	butter or margarine
1 cup	heavy cream
2 cups	grated Parmesan cheese
2 tablespoons	parsley flakes
½ teaspoon	salt
	pepper

In a frying pan, brown chicken until done.

Cook noodles in water according to package directions and drain.

Heat butter and cream in a small saucepan over low heat until butter melts. Stir in remaining ingredients. Top warm noodles with chicken and sauce.

#52

Fajita-Inspired Ramen

MAKES 2 SERVINGS

2	boneless, skinless chicken breasts, cut into strips
1½ cups	sliced onion
1 cup	sliced red or green bell peppers
2 cups	salsa
2 packages	ramen noodles, any flavor
½ cup	sour cream

In a frying pan, brown chicken until done. Add onion, peppers, and salsa and cook over medium heat until vegetables are tender.

Cook noodles in water according to package directions and drain. Serve chicken mixture over warm noodles and top with sour cream.

#53

Italian Chicken

MAKES 2 SERVINGS

2	boneless, skinless chicken breasts, cut into chunks
1 cup	Italian dressing, divided
2 packages	ramen noodles, any flavor

If possible, let chicken marinate overnight in $\frac{1}{2}$ cup dressing.

Cook noodles in water according to package directions and drain.

In a frying pan, cook chicken in the dressing until golden brown. Drizzle remaining $\frac{1}{2}$ cup dressing on noodles and toss. Top with chicken.

Fiesta Chicken

MAKES 2–4 SERVINGS

1 pound	boneless, skinless chicken breasts, cut into chunks
	olive oil
½ cup	corn
½ cup	black beans, drained and rinsed
½ cup	chopped red bell pepper
2 packages	Cajun chicken ramen noodles, with seasoning packets
2 to 3 tablespoons	sour cream
2 tablespoons	salsa

In a frying pan, brown chicken in olive oil. Add corn, black beans, and pepper. Sauté over low heat until heated through and vegetables are tender.

Cook noodles in water according to package directions and drain. Add seasoning packets. Combine noodles with chicken mixture. Stir in sour cream and salsa.

Cheesy Chicken Casserole

MAKES 2 SERVINGS

¼ cup	chopped onion
2 tablespoons	butter or margarine
1 can (10.75 ounces)	condensed cream of chicken soup
½ cup	milk
1 package	chicken ramen noodles, with seasoning packet
1 cup	grated sharp cheddar cheese
1 can (5 ounces)	white chicken chunks, drained

Preheat oven to 350 degrees.

In a saucepan, sauté onion in butter until tender. Add soup, milk, and just under ½ of the seasoning packet. Stir until smooth.

Cook noodles in water according to package directions and drain. Add cheese, chicken, and soup mixture. Stir until cheese is melted. Pour into a 1-quart greased casserole dish and bake 30 minutes.

Chicken 'n' Asparagus

MAKES 4 SERVINGS

4	boneless, skinless chicken breasts
2 packages	chicken ramen noodles, with seasoning packets
2 cans (10.75 ounces each)	condensed cream of asparagus or mushroom soup
1 cup	milk
½ pound	fresh asparagus, cut up
1 cup	grated cheddar cheese

In a frying pan, brown chicken until done. Add noodles, 1 seasoning packet, soup, milk, and asparagus. Simmer over low heat 10 minutes, or until noodles are done. Sprinkle with cheese before serving.

Chinese-Style Ramen

MAKES 2 SERVINGS

½ pound	boneless, skinless chicken breasts, cut into chunks
¼ cup	water chestnut halves
½ cup	snow peas
⅓ cup	bean sprouts
¼ cup	celery
2 to 3 teaspoons	oil
1 package	Oriental ramen noodles, with seasoning packet
1 tablespoon	soy sauce

In a frying pan, brown chicken until done. Add water chestnuts, snow peas, bean sprouts, celery, and oil. Sauté until vegetables are tender.

Cook noodles in water according to package directions and drain. Add seasoning packet. Spoon vegetables over warm noodles and sprinkle with soy sauce.

Chicken Milano

MAKES 2–4 SERVINGS

1 pound	boneless, skinless chicken breasts, cut into chunks
2 teaspoons	minced garlic
1 tablespoon	olive oil
½ cup	chopped sun-dried tomatoes
1 tablespoon	basil
½ cup	chicken broth
2 packages	chicken ramen noodles, with seasoning packets
	salt and pepper, to taste

In a frying pan, brown chicken and garlic in oil until done. Add sun-dried tomatoes, basil, and chicken broth. Simmer over low heat 5 minutes.

Cook noodles in water according to package directions and drain. Add 1 seasoning packet. Serve chicken mixture over warm noodles. Season with salt and pepper.

PORK

All-American Ramen

MAKES 2–4 SERVINGS

2 packages	**ramen noodles, any flavor, with seasoning packets**
¼ cup	**chopped onion**
4	**hot dogs, sliced**
1 cup	**grated cheddar cheese**

Cook noodles in water according to package directions and drain. Add seasoning packets.

In a frying pan, sauté onion and hot dogs together until heated through. Add hot dog mixture to noodles. Add cheese and stir until melted.

Ham and Cheese Ramen Omelets

MAKES 2–4 SERVINGS

2 packages	ramen noodles, any flavor, with seasoning packets
2 tablespoons	butter or margarine
6	eggs, beaten
1 cup	chopped ham
½ cup	chopped onion
½ cup	chopped green bell pepper
½ to 1 cup	grated Swiss cheese

Cook noodles in water according to package directions and drain. Add seasoning packets.

In a frying pan, melt butter, and then add beaten eggs. Fold in noodles and remaining ingredients. Cook until light brown.

#61

Cheesy Bacon Noodles

MAKES 2–4 SERVINGS

2 packages	**ramen noodles, any flavor**
2 cups	**grated cheddar cheese**
½ to 1 cup	**bacon, cooked and crumbled**
	salt and pepper, to taste

Cook noodles in water according to package directions and drain. Add cheese immediately and stir until melted. Stir in bacon and season with salt and pepper.

#62

Brats 'n' Noodles

MAKES 2–4 SERVINGS

2 packages	**ramen noodles, any flavor, with seasoning packets**
4	**bratwursts or cheddarwursts, sliced**

Boil noodles and brats together. Drain and stir in 1 seasoning packet.

Pork and Peppers

MAKES 2 SERVINGS

2	pork chops
1/4 cup	chopped red bell pepper
1/4 cup	chopped green bell pepper
2 tablespoons	chopped onion
1 package	pork ramen noodles, with seasoning packet
2 tablespoons	butter or margarine
2 tablespoons	flour
1 cup	water mixed with seasoning packet
1 tablespoon	vinegar
1/4 teaspoon	tarragon leaves
1/4 teaspoon	thyme leaves

In a frying pan, brown pork chops until done and then remove. Sauté peppers and onion in drippings until tender.

Cook noodles in water according to package directions and drain.

In a small saucepan, heat butter over low heat until light brown. Add flour, stirring until deep brown. Remove from heat. Add remaining ingredients. Heat to boiling and stir 1 minute. Top warm noodles with pork chops and sauce.

Pork Chop Ramen

MAKES 4 SERVINGS

4	pork chops
1 teaspoon	oil
½ cup	sliced onion
1 can (10.75 ounces)	condensed cream of celery soup
½ cup	water
2 packages	pork ramen noodles, with seasoning packets

In a frying pan over medium heat, brown pork chops in oil 5 minutes per side, or until done, and drain. Add onion, soup, and water. Simmer over low heat 10 minutes.

Cook noodles in water according to package directions and drain. Add seasoning packets. Serve pork chops and sauce over warm noodles.

Hungarian-Style Skillet Meal

MAKES 2 SERVINGS

1 package	ramen noodles, any flavor
½ pound	pork strips
1 can (8 ounces)	tomato sauce
¼ cup	onion, thinly sliced
1 teaspoon	paprika
⅓ cup	sour cream

Cook noodles in water according to package directions and drain.

In a frying pan, brown pork until done. Add tomato sauce, onion, paprika, and noodles. Cook over low heat until onion is tender. Stir in noodles. Remove from heat and add sour cream.

Lean Pork Steak

MAKES 2 SERVINGS

2 packages	**pork ramen noodles, with seasoning packets**
2	**lean pork steaks, cut into bite-size pieces**
1 teaspoon	**dried minced onion**
3/4 cup	**water**

Cook noodles in water according to package directions and drain.

In a frying pan, cook steak pieces until done. Add onion, water, and seasoning packets. Simmer, covered, 10 minutes. Stir in noodles and simmer 3–5 minutes more.

Tropical Ramen

MAKES 2 SERVINGS

2 packages	ramen noodles, any flavor
2 cups	cooked ham, cut into strips
1 cup	pineapple chunks
1 cup	crispy Chinese noodles
1 stalk	celery, sliced

Cook noodles in water according to package directions and drain. Rinse with cold water.

Stir in ham, pineapple, crispy noodles, and celery.

SEAFOOD

Cheesy Tuna Ramen
MAKES 2–4 SERVINGS

2 packages	**ramen noodles, any flavor**
2 cans (10.75 ounces each)	**condensed cream of mushroom soup**
1 cup	**milk**
2 cans (5 ounces each)	**tuna, drained**
2 cups	**peas**
2 cups	**grated cheddar cheese**

Cook noodles in water according to package directions and drain. Add soup, milk, tuna, and peas. Simmer 5 minutes. Sprinkle cheese over top and serve.

Tuna Noodle Casserole

MAKES 2–4 SERVINGS

2 cans (5 ounces each)	**tuna, drained**
1 cup	**grated cheddar cheese**
½ cup	**water**
1 cup	**milk**
2	**eggs, beaten**
2 packages	**chicken ramen noodles, broken up, with seasoning packets**
10 to 20	**saltine crackers, crushed**

Preheat oven to 350 degrees.

In a bowl, mix tuna, cheese, water, milk, eggs, and 1 seasoning packet. Transfer mixture to a casserole dish. Add broken uncooked noodles. Bake 15 minutes, stirring occasionally. Sprinkle crackers over top and bake 5 minutes more.

Twice-Baked Tuna Casserole

MAKES 2–4 SERVINGS

2 packages	ramen noodles, any flavor, with seasoning packets
2 cans (5 ounces each)	tuna, drained
1 cup	cheese
½ cup	chopped onion
1 cup	crushed potato chips

Preheat oven to 350 degrees.

Cook noodles in water according to package directions and drain. Season with 1 seasoning packet. Mix tuna, cheese, onion, and noodles together in a small casserole dish and bake 15–20 minutes. Sprinkle chips over top and bake 15 minutes more.

#71

Creamy Mushroom Shrimp Ramen

MAKES 2 SERVINGS

1 package	**Oriental ramen noodles, with seasoning packet**
1 can (10.75 ounces)	**condensed cream of mushroom soup**
1 can (4 ounces)	**shrimp, drained**
1 cup	**sliced fresh mushrooms**

Cook noodles in water according to package directions; do not drain. Add soup, shrimp, mushrooms, and $\frac{1}{2}$ of the seasoning packet. Cook 10 minutes over medium heat.

Cheesy Salmon Noodles

MAKES 2 SERVINGS

1 package	ramen noodles, any flavor
1 can (10.75 ounces)	condensed cream of mushroom soup
½ cup	milk
1 can (5 ounces)	salmon, drained
1 cup	cooked spinach or asparagus
1 cup	grated cheddar cheese

Cook noodles in water according to package directions and drain. Add soup, milk, salmon, and broccoli. Simmer 5 minutes. Sprinkle cheese over top and serve.

Shrimp Ramen

MAKES 2 SERVINGS

1 package	Oriental ramen noodles, with seasoning packet
1 can (10.75 ounces)	condensed cream of celery soup
1 can (4 ounces)	shrimp, drained
	salt and pepper, to taste

Cook noodles in water according to package directions and drain. Add just under ½ of the seasoning packet. Add soup, shrimp, salt, and pepper. Cook 10 minutes over medium heat.

Garlic Shrimp 'n' Veggies
MAKES 2-4 SERVINGS

1	green bell pepper, thinly sliced
1	red bell pepper, thinly sliced
1/2	small onion, thinly sliced
1 1/2 tablespoons	minced garlic
3 to 4 tablespoons	olive oil
2 cups	cooked small shrimp, peeled and deveined
2 packages	Oriental ramen noodles, with seasoning packets

In a frying pan, sauté peppers, onion, and garlic in olive oil until tender. Add shrimp and 1 seasoning packet. Simmer 3–5 minutes.

Cook noodles in water according to package directions and drain. Add 1/2 of remaining seasoning packet. Serve shrimp mixture over noodles.

FAMILY FAVORITES

Ramen Nachos

MAKES 2 SERVINGS

1 package	beef ramen noodles, broken up, with seasoning packet
½ cup	cubed American cheese
1 cup	chili
1 cup	crushed corn chips
	sour cream
1	green onion, chopped

Cook noodles in water according to package directions and drain. Add ½ of the seasoning packet.

In a saucepan, stir warm noodles, cheese, chili, and crushed chips together over low heat until cheese is melted. Garnish with sour cream and green onion.

Garlic Noodle Sauté

MAKES 2–4 SERVINGS

2 packages	**chicken ramen noodles, with seasoning packets**
2 cups	**sliced fresh mushrooms**
½	**red onion, sliced**
1 tablespoon	**minced garlic**
	olive oil

Cook noodles in water according to package directions and drain. Season with 1 seasoning packet.

In a frying pan, sauté mushrooms, onion, and garlic in olive oil until tender. Add warm noodles and sauté 2 minutes.

Creamy Alfredo Noodles

MAKES 2–3 SERVINGS

2 packages	ramen noodles, any flavor
1 cup	butter or margarine
1 cup	cream
2 cups	freshly grated Parmesan cheese
1 teaspoon	garlic salt
	Italian seasoning, to taste
	pepper, to taste

Cook noodles in water according to package directions and drain.

In a saucepan, heat butter and cream over low heat until butter is melted. Stir in remaining ingredients. Simmer sauce 5 minutes. Serve over warm noodles.

Crunchy, Cheesy Casserole

MAKES 2–4 SERVINGS

2 packages	chicken mushroom ramen noodles, with seasoning packets
1 cup	cubed Monterey Jack cheese
½ cup	diced green chilies
¼ cup	sliced black olives
1 cup	sour cream
1 cup	grated cheddar cheese
¼ cup	grated Parmesan cheese
½ cup	crushed corn chips

Preheat oven to 400 degrees.

Cook noodles in water according to package directions; rinse with cold water. Combine noodles, seasoning packets, Monterey Jack cheese, chilies, and olives. Stir in sour cream.

Spoon noodle mixture into a greased casserole dish. Sprinkle with remaining cheeses and chips. Bake 20 minutes, or until brown and bubbly.

Pizza Pasta

MAKES 2–4 SERVINGS

2 packages	ramen noodles, any flavor
2 to 3 cups	spaghetti sauce
20 to 25	pepperoni slices, halved
3/4 cup	chopped green bell pepper
1/2 cup	grated cheddar cheese
1 cup	grated mozzarella cheese

Preheat oven to 350 degrees.

Cook noodles in water according to package directions and drain.

In a saucepan, combine sauce, pepperoni, pepper, and cheddar cheese. Stir constantly until cheese is melted.

Place noodles in a lightly greased 8 x 8-inch pan. Pour sauce mixture over top. Sprinkle with mozzarella cheese. Bake 15 minutes, or until cheese is melted.

Lasagna

MAKES 2–4 SERVINGS

2 packages	**ramen noodles, any flavor**
2 cups	**spaghetti sauce**
1 cup	**ricotta cheese**
1 cup	**grated mozzarella cheese**
1 cup	**Parmesan cheese**

Preheat oven to 350 degrees.

Cook noodles in water according to package directions and drain. Stir sauce into noodles.

In an 8 x 8-inch pan, layer half of the noodle mixture, $\frac{1}{2}$ cup ricotta, $\frac{1}{2}$ cup mozzarella, and $\frac{1}{2}$ cup Parmesan cheeses. Repeat layers. Bake 20 minutes.

Meaty Spaghetti

MAKES 2–4 SERVINGS

2 packages	**ramen noodles, any flavor**
1 to 2 cups	**spaghetti sauce**
1 pound	**ground beef or sausage, browned and drained**
	grated Parmesan cheese

Cook noodles in water according to package directions and drain.

In a saucepan, heat sauce and cooked beef over medium heat 3–5 minutes, or until heated through. Spoon sauce over warm noodles and then sprinkle with cheese.

Primavera Pasta

MAKES 2–4 SERVINGS

1/4 cup	slivered almonds
1 cup	chopped broccoli
1 cup	snow peas
1 cup	sliced red bell pepper
1/2 cup	thinly sliced carrots
1/2 cup	thinly sliced red onion
3 tablespoons	vegetable oil
2 packages	chicken ramen noodles, broken up
1 1/2 cups	water

In a frying pan, toast almonds until lightly browned, and then set aside. Stir-fry vegetables in oil 3–4 minutes. Add broken noodles and water. Steam 3–5 minutes, or until noodles are done, stirring occasionally. Top with toasted almonds to serve.

#83

Parmesan Noodles

MAKES 2–4 SERVINGS

2 packages	**ramen noodles, any flavor**
½ cup	**grated Parmesan cheese**
	salt and pepper, to taste

Cook noodles in water according to package directions and drain. Add Parmesan to warm noodles and stir until cheese is melted. Sprinkle with more Parmesan cheese if desired. Season with salt and pepper.

#84

Cheesy Noodles

MAKES 2–4 SERVINGS

2 packages	**ramen noodles, any flavor**
1 cup	**cubed American processed cheese**
½ to ¾ cup	**milk**
	salt and pepper, to taste

Cook noodles in water according to package directions and drain. Add cheese and milk and stir until cheese is melted. Season with salt and pepper.

Cheesy Ranch Ramen

MAKES 2–4 SERVINGS

2 packages	finely chopped ramen noodles, any flavor
1 cup	ranch dressing
2 cups	grated cheddar cheese

Cook noodles in water according to package directions and drain. Add ranch dressing and cheese to noodles and cook over low heat, stirring constantly, until cheese is melted.

#86

Buttery Chive Noodles

MAKES 2–4 SERVINGS

2 packages	ramen noodles, any flavor
2 tablespoons	butter or margarine
½ cup	chopped chives
	salt and pepper, to taste

Cook noodles in water according to package directions and drain. Add butter to warm noodles and stir until melted. Add chives and season with salt and pepper.

Onion Noodles

MAKES 2 SERVINGS

2 tablespoons	vegetable oil
1 package	ramen noodles, any flavor, broken up
1 can (10.75 ounces)	condensed onion soup
1 soup can	water
1 to 2 tablespoons	chopped chives

Heat oil in a saucepan over medium heat. Add noodles and lightly brown, stirring constantly. Add soup and water. Cover and simmer 10 minutes. Drain noodles and serve with chives sprinkled over top.

Ramen Trail Mix

MAKES 12 CUPS

3 packages	**ramen noodles, any flavor**
15 small sticks	**beef jerky, cut into small pieces**
½ pound	**dried apricots or other dried fruit, cut into small pieces**
½ cup	**dried cranberries, blueberries, cherries, or bananas**
2 cups	**dry roasted peanuts**

Break noodles into a bowl. Add remaining ingredients and stir.

For a more traditional trail mix, omit the beef jerky and fruit. Add 1 pound plain M&Ms, 1 cup raisins, 1 cup sunflower seeds, and 3 cups granola cereal to broken-up noodles and stir.

Ramen Haystacks

MAKES 4–6 SERVINGS

2 cups	**butterscotch chips**
1 tablespoon	**butter**
1 tablespoon	**milk**
1 package	**ramen noodles, any flavor, crumbled**

In a saucepan, heat butterscotch, butter, and milk over low heat until chips are completely melted. Stir crumbled, uncooked noodles into butterscotch mixture until coated. Place spoon-size balls on wax paper, and refrigerate until cool.

#90

Crunchy Chocolate-Coconut Bars

MAKES 6–8 SERVINGS

2 packages	ramen noodles, any flavor
3 cups	milk chocolate chips
2 cups	mini marshmallows
½ cup	coconut
½ cup	chopped walnuts

Preheat oven to 350 degrees.

Do not break noodles. Put blocks of noodles in a lightly greased 8 x 8-inch pan. Cover with layers of chocolate chips and marshmallows. Heat in warm oven until marshmallows and chocolate chips are melted. Layer remaining ingredients over top and refrigerate. When cooled, cut into bars.

Peach Treats

MAKES 2 SERVINGS

1 cup	**cream**
1 can (8.5 ounces)	**peaches, drained with juice reserved**
¼ cup	**brown sugar**
1 package	**ramen noodles, any flavor, crushed**
½ cup	**crushed Frosted Flakes**

Preheat oven to 350 degrees.

In a small casserole dish, mix cream, peaches and ½ cup of their juices, and brown sugar. Add crushed noodles, making sure they are completely covered by cream mixture. Bake 5 minutes. Sprinkle Frosted Flakes over top and bake 5 minutes more.

Maple and Brown Sugar Ramenmeal

MAKES 2 SERVINGS

1 package	ramen noodles, any flavor
1 cup	milk
1 tablespoon	maple syrup
1 tablespoon	brown sugar

Crumble ramen into a microwave-safe bowl. Pour in milk, syrup, and brown sugar. Microwave on high 4 minutes, stirring occasionally.

If you'd rather have something fruity, omit the syrup and sugar and add 1 sliced banana, 1 cup blueberries, or a mixture of $\frac{1}{2}$ diced apples, 1 teaspoon cinnamon, and 1 tablespoon sugar.

VEGETABLE ENTRÉES

Broccoli-Cauliflower Ramen

MAKES 2 SERVINGS

1 can (10.75 ounces)	condensed cream of celery soup
½ cup	milk
1 cup	broccoli pieces
½ cup	cauliflower pieces
½ cup	sliced carrots
1 package	ramen noodles, any flavor, with seasoning packet

In a saucepan, heat soup and milk to boiling. Stir in vegetables and heat to boiling. Reduce heat and simmer 15 minutes.

Cook noodles in water according to package directions and drain. Add seasoning packet. Top warm noodles with soup mixture.

Cheesy Vegetable Ramen

MAKES 2 SERVINGS

1 package	ramen noodles, any flavor, with seasoning packet
1 cup	frozen mixed vegetables
1 tablespoon	water
1 small jar	creamy cheese sauce, condensed

Cook noodles in water according to package directions and drain. Add $1/2$ of the seasoning packet and set aside.

In a frying pan, cook vegetables in water until tender. Add cheese sauce to vegetables and heat through. Stir in noodles.

Hollandaise Vegetable Noodles

MAKES 2 SERVINGS

1 package	chicken ramen noodles, with seasoning packet
2	egg yolks
3 tablespoons	lemon juice
½ cup	butter or margarine
1 cup	fresh or frozen mixed vegetables

Cook noodles in water according to package directions and drain.

In a saucepan, whisk egg yolks and lemon juice briskly with a fork. Add ½ of the butter and stir over low heat until melted. Add remaining butter, stirring briskly until melted and sauce thickens. Cook vegetables and drain. Top warm noodles with vegetables and sauce.

Veggie Sauté

MAKES 2 SERVINGS

1 package	ramen noodles, any flavor, with seasoning packet
½ cup	sliced onion
½ cup	diced tomato
1 can (4 ounces)	mushrooms, drained
½ cup	chopped green bell pepper
1 teaspoon	garlic powder
2 tablespoons	oil

Cook noodles in water according to package directions and drain. Season noodles with ½ of the seasoning packet.

In a frying pan, sauté vegetables in garlic powder and oil over low heat until tender. Stir in warm noodles.

Chinese-Style Fried Noodles

MAKES 2–4 SERVINGS

2 packages	Oriental ramen noodles, with seasoning packets
1 cup	frozen peas and carrots
2	eggs
1 to 2 teaspoons	oil
2 to 3 tablespoons	soy sauce

Cook noodles in water according to package directions and drain. Add seasoning packets. Heat vegetables in microwave until heated through and add to warm noodles.

In a frying pan, fry eggs in oil; break yolk and cook until hard, flipping occasionally. Cut eggs into small pieces. Stir into noodle mixture. Sprinkle soy sauce over top and stir together, adding more if necessary.

Tomato Sauté

MAKES 2–4 SERVINGS

2 packages	ramen noodles, any flavor, with seasoning packets
1 cup	butter or margarine
2 cans (14.5 ounces each)	diced tomatoes
2 teaspoons	minced garlic
	salt and pepper, to taste

Cook noodles in water according to package directions and drain.

In a frying pan, melt butter. Add tomatoes, garlic, seasoning packets, and noodles and stir. Season with salt and pepper. Simmer 5 minutes.

Garlic and Cilantro Noodles

MAKES 2–4 SERVINGS

2 packages	**Oriental ramen noodles, with seasoning packets**
2 cups	**fresh or frozen mixed vegetables**
1 teaspoon	**minced garlic**
2 tablespoons	**fresh chopped cilantro**

Cook noodles and mixed vegetables in water together and drain. Add garlic, cilantro, and seasoning packets. Simmer over low heat 5 minutes, stirring occasionally.

Creamy Corn and Cheese Noodles

MAKES 2 SERVINGS

1 package	ramen noodles, any flavor, with seasoning packet
1½ cups	grated cheddar cheese
1 can (14 ounces)	creamed corn

Cook noodles in water according to package directions and drain. Add seasoning packet.

In a saucepan, heat cheese and corn over medium heat, stirring occasionally, until the cheese is melted. Mix with warm noodles.

Soy Sauce Veggie Noodles

MAKES 2 SERVINGS

1 package	**Oriental ramen noodles, with seasoning packet**
1 cup	**frozen stir-fry vegetables**
1½ teaspoons	**olive oil**
1 tablespoon	**soy sauce**
	salt and pepper, to taste

Cook noodles in water according to package directions and drain. Add seasoning packet.

In a frying pan, sauté vegetables in olive oil until heated through, then add to warm noodles. Sprinkle soy sauce over top and stir together. Season with salt and pepper.

NOTES

NOTES

NOTES

NOTES

NOTES

NOTES

NOTES

NOTES

Metric Conversion Chart

VOLUME MEASUREMENTS		WEIGHT MEASUREMENTS		TEMPERATURE CONVERSION	
U.S.	Metric	U.S.	Metric	Fahrenheit	Celsius
1 teaspoon	5 ml	1/2 ounce	15 g	250	120
1 tablespoon	15 ml	1 ounce	30 g	300	150
1/4 cup	60 ml	3 ounces	90 g	325	160
1/3 cup	75 ml	4 ounces	115 g	350	180
1/2 cup	125 ml	8 ounces	225 g	375	190
2/3 cup	150 ml	12 ounces	350 g	400	200
3/4 cup	175 ml	1 pound	450 g	425	220
1 cup	250 ml	2 1/4 pounds	1 kg	450	230

MORE 101 THINGS® IN THESE
FAVORITES

BACON
CAKE MIX
CASSEROLE
SLOW COOKER
SMOKER

Each 128 pages, $12.99

Gibbs Smith

About the Author

Toni Patrick is the culinary creative behind the wildly successful *101 Things to Do With Ramen Noodles*, as well as several other titles in the popular 101 Things® series, including *101 Things to Do With Mac & Cheese* and *101 More Things to Do With Ramen Noodles*. She has been featured on the Food Network and lives in Greeley, Colorado.